The Little Book of

Calm

Felicity Forster

SIRIUS

SIRIUS

This edition published in 2025 by Sirius Publishing, a division of
Arcturus Publishing Limited,
25/27 Bickels Yard, 151–153 Bermondsey Street,
London SE1 3HA

Copyright © Arcturus Holdings Limited

All rights reserved. No part of this publication may be reproduced, stored
in a retrieval system, or transmitted, in any form or by any means,
electronic, mechanical, photocopying, recording or otherwise, without
prior written permission in accordance with the provisions of the
Copyright Act 1956 (as amended). Any person or persons who do any
unauthorised act in relation to this publication may be liable to criminal
prosecution and civil claims for damages.

ISBN: 978-1-3988-5774-2
AD012760NT

Printed in China

INTRODUCTION

In today's fast-paced world, we're constantly being bombarded with information and stimulation that demands our attention. Emails arrive – ping! – our phones light up with notifications – ding ding!! – and we face obstacles everywhere we look. The bus is delayed, it starts raining, our boss needs something we haven't started yet, the house is a mess, our children are calling, the dishes need doing... the list goes on. In a hyper-stimulating environment like this, our nervous system is constantly in arousal mode. We're fighting fires, trying to stay on top of the ever-present noise of the external world.

This, of course, is not healthy. Left unaddressed, it causes anxiety and stress, and even the feeling that we are not in control of our lives. The antidote is to learn a

few tried-and-tested techniques for restoring calm. It may not be the same for everyone, but once you've established some reliable methods that work for you, you're in a much better position to deal with life's challenges.

This little book of calm contains some inspirational quotes and go-to practices that are designed to bring calmness into your life. Deep breathing is often a good place to start – it activates the parasympathetic nervous system and works for most people. Other strategies include stroking a pet, doing arts and crafts and embracing the Danish tradition of hygge. Music has a powerful role to play too, as do quiet pursuits such as meditation, reading and spending time in nature. With practice, it's possible to develop an ability to keep calm in any situation.

'Breath is the power behind all things…. I breathe in and know that good things will happen.'

Tao Porchon-Lynch

'The greatest weapon against stress is our ability to choose one thought over another.'

William James

Take a moment to...
breathe

When we begin to feel anxious, it can make our hearts thump, send our pulses racing and just breathing can feel difficult. Try these simple steps to help regain control:

❶ Sit or stand, and let your arms relax on the arms of your chair or by your sides.

❷ Breathe slowly in, aiming to fill your lungs without forcing the air in.

❸ Then breathe slowly out, focusing on the air as it leaves your body.

❹ Ignore sounds around you, and if possible and safe to do so, close your eyes to help you focus on your breathing. If it helps, try counting as you breathe in and out.

❺ Repeat this slow breathing for about 5 minutes until you feel more relaxed.

'The nearer a man comes to a calm mind the closer he is to strength.'

Marcus Aurelius

'The best entrepreneurs aren't frazzled; they're not tactic chasers. They're calm. They're systematic and they learn to say no.'

Ramit Sethi

'Your calm mind is the ultimate weapon against your challenges. So relax.'

Bryant McGill

Stroke a pet

Pets love being stroked, and the calming effect goes both ways – there's nothing as calming as a cat's purr! It has been shown that when we pet an animal, it releases our body's natural pain relievers, lowers our heart rate and decreases our blood pressure. Bonding with an animal can also reduce feelings of loneliness and anxiety.

❶ Take the time to work out what your pet likes best. Hold out your hand first and let the animal determine the pace.

❷ Dogs often like back strokes and belly rubs, while cats may prefer strokes along the sides of the face, under the chin and behind the ears.

❸ If you don't own a pet, visit a petting zoo where you're allowed to touch a variety of friendly farmyard animals.

'A wild person with a calm mind can make anything.'

Eric Maisel

'Calm is the magic elixir that brings you to a place of balance, harmony, and peace.'

Donald Altman

'Peace is the result of retraining your mind to process life as it is, rather than as you think it should be.'

Wayne W. Dyer

Visualize a safe place

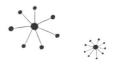

Picturing yourself in a peaceful and safe place is a really easy way to feel calm. Learning the skill of visualization allows you to stop focusing on whatever is making you anxious and transfer your mind to a new set of thoughts that will calm you down. It takes a bit of practice.

❶ Choose your safe place. Many people like to think of a beach with gentle waves lapping the shore, but it could be anywhere – a park, a forest, a room, or an imaginary place such as underwater or above the clouds.

❷ Sit or lie somewhere comfortable with no distractions.

❸ Close your eyes, relax, and imagine yourself in your safe place. Think about every detail: the sounds, sights, smells and feelings.

❹ You could go further with your visualization by imagining you're an object in your safe place, such as a small stone. With practice, you'll be able to set your worries aside and 'become' the little stone quite quickly.

'90% of what you're stressing about right now won't even matter a year from now. Take a deep breath.'

Mel Robbins

'Worry never robs tomorrow of its sorrow, it only saps today of its joy.'

Leo F. Buscaglia

Count sheep

This isn't an old wives' tale! Counting sheep (or counting anything at all) actually does help us fall asleep. The theory is that counting distracts our racing mind when we're trying to relax, refocusing our attention away from stressful worries towards a relaxing rhythm of calm thoughts.

❶ Close your eyes and imagine a large group of sheep near a fence.

❷ Count each sheep as it jumps over the fence.

❸ If you prefer, forget the sheep and simply count backwards from 100.

❹ An alternative distraction technique is to play word games in your head, such as thinking of items around the house that begin with each letter of the alphabet.

'Cultivate outward calm and inward calm will come.'

Obi-Wan Kenobi

'A crust eaten in peace is better than a banquet partaken in anxiety.'

Aesop

'Tension is who you think you should be. Relaxation is who you are.'

Chinese proverb

Practise hygge

The Danish tradition of *hygge* (pronounced 'hoo-guh') epitomizes cosiness, contentment, comfort and conviviality. It's all about feeling nurtured by the simple things and creating a welcoming atmosphere of warmth.

❶ One of the easiest ways to create *hygge* is to light candles around your home and enjoy their soft, ambient glow.

❷ Hang fairy lights around window frames or in trees.

❸ Enjoy time with family and friends – chat quietly together on blankets after dark, or cosy up to watch a movie together.

❹ Savour comforting drinks such as hot chocolate or mulled wine.

'Slow down, calm down, don't worry, don't hurry. Trust the process.'

Alexandra Stoddard

'Inner peace is beyond victory or defeat.'

Bhagavad Gita

'It's not stress that kills us, it is our reaction to it.'

Hans Selye

Try the 54321 method

Using a grounding technique such as the 54321 method is a way of redirecting anxious thoughts into calm contemplation. The idea is to anchor all five of our senses to the present moment. Go slowly through each step, counting down from 5 and looking for:

1. Five things you can see.
2. Four things you can touch.
3. Three things you can hear.
4. Two things you can smell.
5. One thing you can taste.

'If the mind is calm, your spontaneity and honest thoughts appear. You become more spontaneous.'

Chade-Meng Tan

'Quiet mind, quiet soul.'

Lailah Gifty Akita

'And it is the mind that can learn to stay calm, resourceful, compassionate, and effective. Everything depends on our state of mind – the one thing in life we can do something about.'

Eknath Easwaran

Colour a mandala

The word 'mandala' comes from the Sanskrit for 'circle', and Buddhists traditionally make these with coloured sand, creating beautiful and intricate works of art which are then swept away to signify that nothing lasts. Drawing and colouring are great ways to reduce the chatter in our heads and keep our attention in the present moment.

❶ Create a mandala by drawing a small circle in the middle of a page.

❷ Working your way outwards, add petal shapes, triangles and circles to build up your design. Fill in the mandala with zig-zags, stripes or dots.

❸ Colour in your mandala using any colours you wish.

❹ You could also buy a book of mandalas for colouring in, or download patterns from the internet.

'Well, I can't eat muffins in an agitated manner. The butter would probably get on my cuffs. One should always eat muffins quite calmly. It is the only way to eat them.'

Oscar Wilde

'I have to stay calm, cool, and collected.'

Canelo Alvarez

Relax your muscles

A technique known as progressive muscle relaxation (PMR) is a process in which you systematically tense each muscle group, then relax it. Once you can distinguish easily between the feeling of a tense muscle and a relaxed one, you can begin to initiate relaxation at the first sign of tension.

❶ Set aside about 15 minutes and sit somewhere comfortable and warm. Take a few deep breaths.

❷ Start with whichever muscle you wish to target. Many people like to start with their feet and work their way up. Squeeze the muscle as hard as you can for 5 seconds.

❸ Then quickly relax the muscle. Make an effort to notice the difference between tension and relaxation.

❹ Repeat the process all the way up to your head, raising your eyebrows as high as you can, then relaxing them.

'Calm self-confidence is as far from conceit as the desire to earn a decent living is remote from greed.'

Channing Pollock

'Within you, there is a stillness and a sanctuary to which you can retreat at any time and be yourself.'

Hermann Hesse

'There's a lot more power in calm than in vituperation.'

Dennis Prager

Go for a
walk

Walking is not only good exercise, it's also great for our mental wellbeing. It keeps us alert, boosts our mood and reduces stress and anxiety, and can also improve our social connections if we meet people along the way.

❶ Explore your local area and ideally find somewhere with trees, such as a park or woodland.

❷ Aim to walk for around 30 minutes a day.

❸ Start slowly and build up your pace and distance as you get fitter.

'You don't have to control your thoughts. You just have to stop letting them control you.'

Dan Millman

'The more tranquil a man becomes, the greater is his success, his influence, his power for good. Calmness of mind is one of the beautiful jewels of wisdom.'

James Allen

'Tranquillity is found by abandoning our desires for things that are not in our control and focusing our efforts on those things that are in our control.'

Marc Libre

Meditate

Meditation is a very powerful tool. It allows us to pause and breathe, improving our physical and mental wellbeing. It can reduce anxiety, fears, worries, depression, anger and even grief, and gives us the time and space we need to process our thoughts and emotions.

❶ Set aside about 20 minutes and find somewhere comfortable, quiet and warm to sit.

❷ Be mindful of your surroundings. Focus on the feeling of the chair, the sounds and smells in the room and the temperature of the air.

❸ Close your eyes. Inhale slowly, thinking 'breathe in' as you do so. Then exhale slowly and think 'breathe out'.

❹ Repeat for the next 20 minutes, and whenever you feel distracted by a random thought, consciously bring your mind back to your breath.

'A samurai must remain calm at all times even in the face of danger.'

Chris Bradford

'You wouldn't worry so much about what others think of you if you realized how seldom they do.'

Eleanor Roosevelt

'Smile, breathe, and go slowly.'

Thich Nhat Hanh

Try yoga

Yoga has been around for centuries, and is a great way to relax and recharge both mind and body. It can improve concentration while simultaneously reducing symptoms of anxiety, depression and stress. There are many different types of yoga to choose from:

❶ Restorative yoga focuses on relaxation and stillness. Asanas (poses) are held for several minutes.

❷ Hatha yoga combines asanas with breathing exercises (pranayama).

❸ Yin yoga improves flexibility by stretching and holding poses for a longer amount of time.

❹ Yoga nidra (yogic sleep) is a combination of body scans, breathwork and visualization to achieve a deep form of meditation somewhere between waking and sleeping.

❺ Vinyasa yoga is more dynamic, involving rhythmic and continuous movement.

'Everything we do is infused with the energy with which we do it. If we're frantic, life will be frantic. If we're peaceful, life will be peaceful.'

Marianne Williamson

'Relax. No one else knows what they're doing either.'

Ricky Gervais

Appreciate nature

Communing with nature, whether spending time outdoors in green spaces or bringing nature into our homes is beneficial to our mental and physical wellbeing, inducing feelings of calm, peace and serenity. There are many ways to appreciate nature:

❶ Instead of spending your lunchtime at your desk, go for a walk in a nearby park.

❷ Notice the birds. Get out of bed early and listen to the dawn chorus, or go for a dusk walk in the countryside where you may be lucky enough to witness a murmuration of birds settling down to roost for the evening.

❸ Grow plants, shrubs, trees and flowers, either in the garden or in indoor pots.

❹ Watch a sunrise or sunset, or sit outside at night and look up at the stars.

'To experience peace doesn't mean that your life is always blissful. It means that you are capable of tapping into a blissful state of mind amidst the normal chaos of a hectic life.'

Jill Bolte Taylor

'Nothing gives one person so much advantage over another as to remain always cool and unruffled under all circumstances.'

Thomas Jefferson

'There are times when we stop, we sit still. We listen and breezes from a whole other world begin to whisper.'

James Carroll

Play!

Playing games and doing puzzles is a fun way to keep calm while stimulating our senses, engaging our mind and keeping anxiety at bay. Here are a few ideas:

❶ Do a jigsaw puzzle – the more difficult, the better!

❷ Buy books of crosswords, wordsearch puzzles, brain teasers, sudoku, mazes, dot-to-dot drawings, spot-the-difference pictures and memory games.

❸ Play card games with friends and family.

❹ Play games on your phone or computer.

'Wisdom yields calmness.'

Paul Graham

'The power for creating a better future is contained in the present moment: You create a good future by creating a good present.'

Eckhart Tolle

'To be calm is the highest achievement of the self.'

Zen proverb

Practise mindfulness

Mindfulness is a way of being present in the moment while calmly accepting our feelings and thoughts. It improves our emotional wellbeing and redirects our energy away from problems and things we cannot control. There are many ways of achieving a state of mindfulness. Here are a few ideas:

❶ Pick up a leaf and imagine you've never seen a leaf before. Make a conscious effort to notice everything about it – the way it looks, its colour, shape, texture, how it feels in your hand and its smell.

❷ Look out the window and pay close attention to everything you can see. Try to avoid naming things; just notice the colours, shapes, patterns and textures.

❸ Next time you have a drink, do so slowly and mindfully. Concentrate on the mug or glass, then focus on the smell of the drink and the taste and texture of it on your tongue.

'In the end, just three things matter: How well we have lived. How well we have loved. How well we have learned to let go.'

Jack Kornfield

'A man of calm is like a shady tree. People who need shelter come to it.'

Toba Beta

'Sometimes you just have to calm down a little bit and let the system work itself.'

Blake Griffin

Get crafty

When we spend time creating something, we are expressing ourselves in a positive way and our brain is occupied doing an activity we enjoy. Art and craft hobbies are great for redirecting our attention away from stressful thoughts.

1. Learn how to knit, crochet or sew. The motions of working the stitches or threads are mesmerizing and calming.

2. Collect leaves or flowers and press them into a journal.

3. Do a painting or drawing.

4. Make a paper collage. Use postcards, magazines or newspaper cuttings to create figures or landscapes, or make abstract mood boards.

5. Sculpt something out of modelling clay.

'It is not enough to win a war; it is more important to organize the peace.'

Aristotle

'Each one has to find his peace from within. And peace to be real must be unaffected by outside circumstances.'

Mahatma Gandhi

Do a body scan meditation

Mentally running through each part of our body and paying attention to how each area feels is an effective way of redirecting our focus from the outside world to our inner world. It makes us feel more connected to our physical and emotional self.

❶ Lie comfortably on your back with your palms facing upwards.

❷ Concentrate on your breathing, noticing its rhythm.

❸ Think about how your clothing feels, the temperature of your body and the room, and the texture of the surface you're lying on.

❹ Start at your feet and focus on each part of your body, moving slowly upwards. Does anything feel light, tingly or tense?

❺ You might find it helpful to imagine your awareness as liquid filling a mould.

'Don't underestimate the value of Doing Nothing, of just going along, listening to all the things you can't hear, and not bothering.'

A. A. Milne

'It's all about finding the calm in the chaos.'

Donna Karan

'Nothing can bring you peace but yourself.'

Ralph Waldo Emerson

Go forest bathing

First coined as *shinrin-yoku* in Japan in the 1980s, forest bathing is a mindfulness practice that offers a relaxing and meaningful antidote to technology burnout, encouraging us to reconnect with nature and improve our mental wellbeing. Being around trees restores our energy and refreshes our mind.

1. Choose a location with trees. It might be a forest or a local park. Leave your phone behind (or at least switch it off).

2. Focus on your five senses. Let nature in through your eyes, ears, nose, mouth, hands and feet – the shapes and colours of the leaves, the birds singing, the leaves rustling, the taste of the air.

3. Feel your surroundings – hug a tree, breathe in deeply, dip your fingers into running water.

4. Stay there for as long as you can. Around 2 hours generally gets the best results.

'Just when the caterpillar thought the world was ending, he turned into a butterfly.'

Proverb

'Trust yourself. You've survived a lot, and you'll survive whatever is coming.'

Robert Tew

'Stress is an ignorant state. It believes that everything is an emergency. Nothing is that important.'

Natalie Goldberg

Play with a
sensory toy

Sensory toys are a simple and fun way of easing stress and promoting calm. They can be used by children and adults alike; they're often recommended for people with concentration issues such as ADHD (attention-deficit/hyperactivity disorder). Here are a few to choose from:

❶ Stress balls, squishies and kneadable doughs.

❷ Fidget spinners and fidget cubes.

❸ Worry beads.

❹ Tangles.

'When in doubt, chill out.'

Tim Fargo

'When I let go of what I am,
I become what I might be.'

Lao Tzu

'When playing music, it is possible to achieve a unique sense of peace.'

Daniel Barenboim

Listen to relaxing music

Calming music is scientifically proven to lower our heart rate, deepen our breathing and reduce feelings of anxiety. It's even been shown that listening to gentle music before surgery can actually result in the need for less sedative.

1. In the world of classical music, choose relaxing instrumental pieces such as Debussy's *Clair de lune* or Chopin's *Nocturnes*.

2. Contemplative film scores can also be really effective. Try Vangelis's *Blade Runner*, Hans Zimmer's *Interstellar* or Alexandre Desplat's *The Shape of Water*.

3. Soothing pop songs include Radiohead's *Everything in its Right Place*, Celine Dion's *The Prayer* and Ed Sheeran's *Perfect*.

4. There are plenty of relaxing music apps and YouTube videos of ambient music that last for hours.

'Anxiety does not empty tomorrow of its sorrows, but only empties today of its strength.'

Charles Spurgeon

'Your mind will answer most questions if you learn to relax and wait for the answer.'

William S. Burroughs

Unwind in
water

Being in water has a powerful effect on our mental health, impacting all five senses at once and giving us a completely immersive, calming experience. Even the colour blue has a positive and relaxing effect.

❶ Swim in a heated pool or luxuriate in a hot tub while being massaged with jets of aerated water.

❷ Take a long hot bath, perhaps adding a few drops of bath oil or a fizzing bath bomb.

❸ Try cold water swimming too! Taking an outdoor dip in the ocean or a lake induces calmness, clarity and feelings of wellbeing, and is known to help with depression.

'When people ask me what the most important thing is in life, I answer: "Just breathe."'

Yoko Ono

'Peace comes from within. Do not seek it without.'

Siddhārtha Gautama

'Calmness is the cradle of power.'

Josiah Gilbert Holland

Lose yourself
in a book

Reading can transport us to other worlds and helps us to relax and de-stress. What could be more calming than curling up in your favourite armchair with a hot drink and good book?

❶ Most of us have a favourite book, perhaps something we first read at school. Do some research and find out what else that author has written.

❷ Visit bookshops and go online to pick up new ideas. Personal recommendations are often a good way to discover new authors.

❸ Read non-fiction too. Choose any subject that you enjoy, whether it's travel, cooking or mountain climbing!

'The day she let go of the things that were weighing her down, was the day she began to shine the brightest.'

Katrina Mayer

'The secret of success is to be in harmony with existence, to be always calm, to let each wave of life wash us a little farther up the shore.'

Cyril Connolly

'Learning to ignore things is one of the great paths to inner peace.'

Robert J. Sawyer

Pamper yourself

Spending a day (or even just a couple of hours) pampering yourself at a spa or wellness resort is the ultimate in relaxation and self-care. You can sign up for any number of wellness therapies and soothing treatments, all provided in a serene and tranquil atmosphere.

❶ A massage eases tight muscles throughout your body and lowers your heart rate and blood pressure.

❷ A facial cleanses and exfoliates your skin while relaxing the muscles in your face and neck.

❸ Aromatherapy uses essential oils such as lavender, eucalyptus, peppermint and tea tree to improve spiritual and emotional wellbeing.

❹ Swimming in warm water supports your weight, soothes tired muscles and helps with injuries.

'To understand the immeasurable, the mind must be extraordinarily quiet, still.'

J. Krishnamurti

'I never let myself get psyched out. My motto is, "Stay calm and carry on."'

Mary Cain

'Learn to be calm and you will always be happy.'

Paramahansa Yogananda

Establish a bedtime routine

Doing the same things in the same order every evening trains your brain to know when it's time for sleep. The following healthy rituals will prime your body to relax and wind down.

❶ Decide on a set bedtime, allowing for around 7–8 hours' sleep.

❷ Keep your bedroom cool, dark and quiet.

❸ Switch off all electronic devices an hour before you go to bed. The blue light they emit tricks your brain into thinking it's daytime.

❹ Take a warm bath, listen to calming music or read a book.

❺ Close your eyes and practise deep breathing or other forms of meditation.

'Understand this and be free:
we are not in our bodies;
our bodies are inside us.'

Sean A. Mulvihil

'It's always the mind that needs quietening and the heart that needs listening to.'

Rasheed Ogunlaru

Listen to
soothing sounds

Sudden loud noises cause us to jump and get ready for action, and conversely, gentle background sounds with soothing rhythms and patterns can promote a sense of calm and relaxation. Many of the following can be found in AI-generated videos and phone apps.

❶ White noise contains all audible frequencies. It sounds like the static from an untuned radio, and is very effective at masking other sounds.

❷ Binaural beats (perceiving a single tone when a different tone is played in each ear) are said to reduce anxiety and even help manage pain.

❸ The sound of water gives us peace, whether it's ocean waves crashing against a beach, the pitter-patter of rain hitting a roof or the gentle splashing of water in a pebbled stream.

❹ A crackling fire in a cosy cottage with the wind blowing or snow falling outside also promotes comfort and relaxation.

'We must be willing to let go of the life we've planned, so as to have the life that is waiting for us.'

Joseph Campbell

'Keep calm and carry on.'

Winston Churchill

'Never be in a hurry; do everything quietly and in a calm spirit. Do not lose your inner peace for anything whatsoever, even if your whole world seems upset.'

Ralph Waldo Emerson

Enjoy a calming hot drink

There are many hot drinks that promote calmness and relaxation. Experiment with whichever ones work for you, and try them when you feel stressed during the day or when you're getting ready for bed. Avoid caffeine and energy drinks when you want to sleep.

1. Chamomile has been used as a medicinal herb for centuries to improve sleep and reduce anxiety. It makes a soothing cup of tea.

2. Valerian is also used to make tea. It has mild sedative properties.

3. Warm milk contains high levels of tryptophan, a neurotransmitter that boosts mood.

4. A mug of hot cocoa or hot chocolate can be comforting and relaxing (but beware of too much sugar and caffeine).

'Calmness yields happiness.'

Maxime Lagacé

'After a storm comes a calm.'

Matthew Henry